Contents

2
Painted Eggs

6
Puzzled

10
Belt Buckles

14
Greys on Pink

18
Five C's

22
Additional Designs
Echoes 22
English Garden 24
Barrell of Monkeys 26
Flower Power 28
Southwest 30
Zigzag 32

34
General Instructions

35
My Designs Blank Chart

36
Yarn Information

MOSAIC ART AFGHANS

Granny squares have been a beloved tradition with crocheters for over 100 years! Traditional granny squares were made with alternating rounds of bold colors and black, giving the afghan a stained-glass look.

Donna Williams has broken away from tradition with her graphic granny designs! Using only one-color and two-color squares, you can make five dramatic afghans or use the additional variations or blank chart to inspire you to create your own special design!

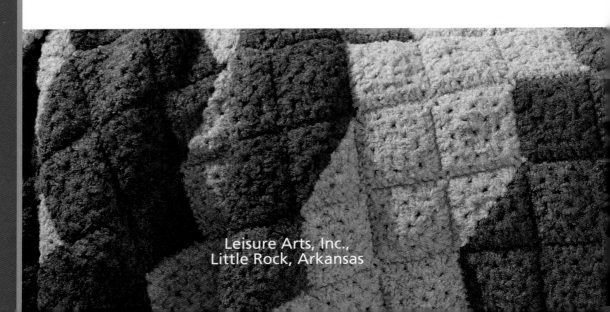

Leisure Arts, Inc.,
Little Rock, Arkansas

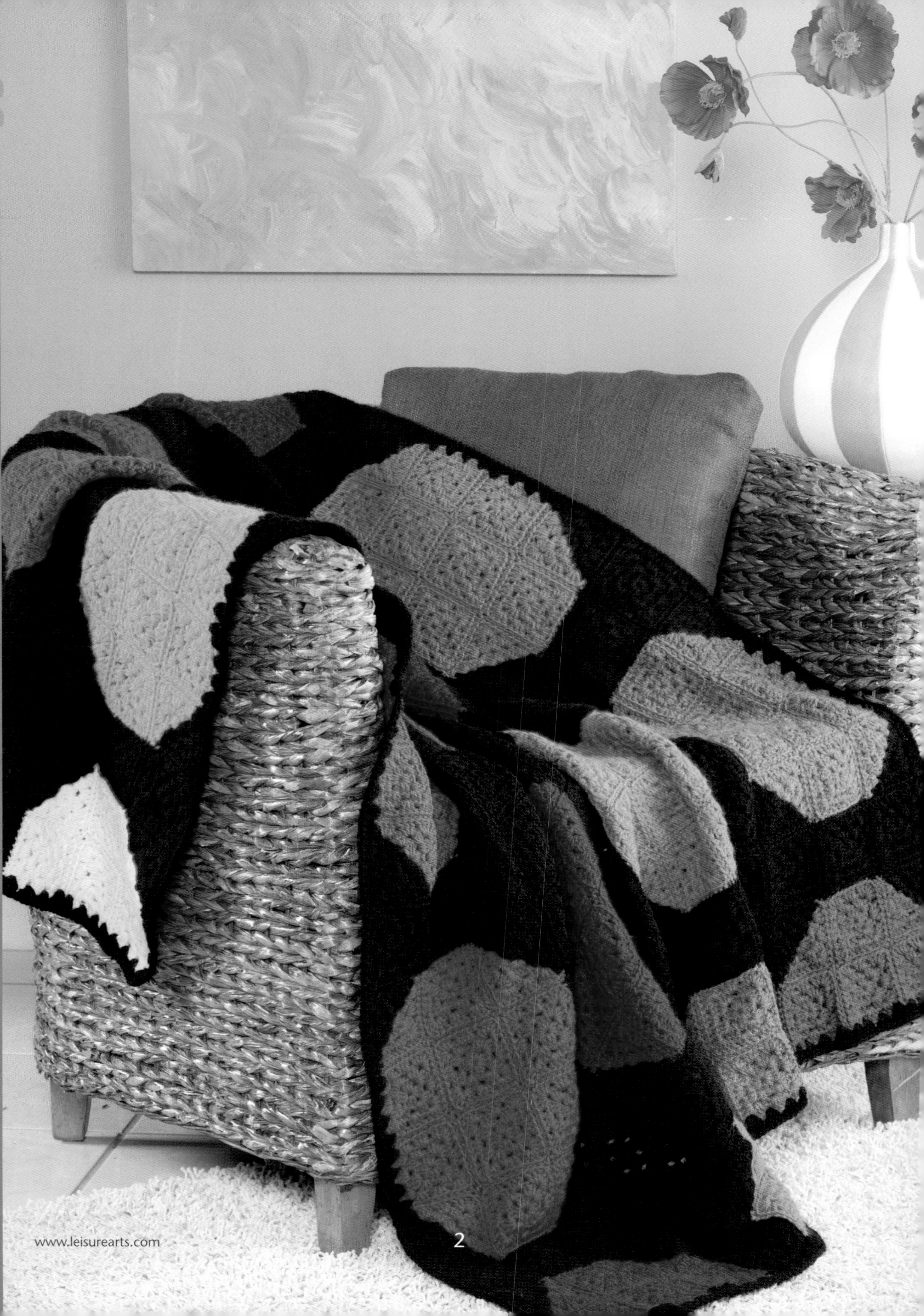

Painted Eggs

◖■▢▷ **EASY**

Finished Size: Approximately 46" x 61"
(117 cm x 155 cm)

MATERIALS
Medium Weight Yarn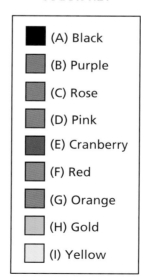
    [3 ounces, 197 yards
    (85 grams, 180 meters) per skein]:
        Black (A) - 8 skein
        Purple (B) - 1 skein
        Rose (C) - 1 skein
        Pink (D) - 2 skeins
        Cranberry (E) - 2 skeins
        Red (F) - 2 skeins
        Orange (G) - 2 skeins
        Gold (H) - 1 skein
        Yellow (I) - 1 skein
Crochet hook, size G (4 mm) **or** size needed
    for gauge
Yarn needle

GAUGE
One Square = 3" (7.5 cm)

ONE-COLOR SQUARE
**Make 108 with Color A, 4 with Color B, 12 with
Color C, 20 with Color D, 28 with Color E, 28 with
Color F, 20 with Color G, 12 with Color H and 4
with Color I.**

Ch 4, join with a slip st to form a ring.

Rnd 1 (Right side): Ch 3 **(counts as first dc, now
and throughout)**, 2 dc in ring; (ch 1, 3 dc in ring) 3
times; sc in first dc to form last ch-1 sp.

Rnd 2: Ch 3, 2 dc in last ch-1 sp made, ★ (3 dc,
ch 1, 3 dc) in next ch-1 sp; rep from ★ 2 times
more, 3 dc in same sp as first dc; sc in first dc to
form last ch-1 sp.

Rnd 3: Ch 3, 2 dc in last ch-1 sp made, ★ skip next
3 dc, 3 dc in sp **before** next dc *(Fig. 1, page 36)*,
(3 dc, ch 1, 3 dc) in next ch-1 sp; rep from ★
2 times **more**, 3 dc in sp **before** next dc, 3 dc in
same sp as first dc, ch 1; join with slip st to first dc,
finish off leaving a long end for sewing.

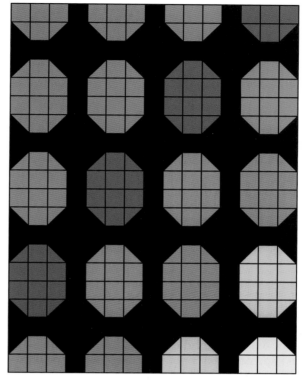

CHART   *15 x 20 squares*

COLOR KEY

■	(A) Black
■	(B) Purple
■	(C) Rose
■	(D) Pink
■	(E) Cranberry
■	(F) Red
■	(G) Orange
■	(H) Gold
■	(I) Yellow

TWO-COLOR SQUARE

Note: All Two-color squares are made with Color A and one other color.

Make 2 with Color A and Color B, 6 with Color A and Color C, 10 with Color A and Color D, 14 with Color A and Color E, 14 with Color A and Color F, 10 with Color A and Color G, 6 with Color A and Color H, and 2 with Color A and Color I.

With Color A, ch 4, join with a slip st to form a ring.

Rnd 1 (Right side): Ch 3, 2 dc in ring, ch 1, 3 dc in ring; drop Color A, with second color, ch 1, (3 dc, ch 1) twice in ring; join with slip st to first dc.

Rnd 2: With second color, ch 3, turn; 2 dc in first ch-1 sp, (3 dc, ch 1, 3 dc) in next ch-1 sp, 3 dc in next ch-1 sp; drop second color, with Color A, ch 1, 3 dc in same sp, (3 dc, ch 1, 3 dc) in next ch-1 sp, 3 dc in same sp as first dc, ch 1; join with slip st to first dc.

Rnd 3: With Color A, ch 3, turn; 2 dc in first ch-1 sp, skip next 3 dc, 3 dc in sp **before** next dc, (3 dc, ch 1, 3 dc) in next ch-1 sp, skip next 3 dc, 3 dc in sp **before** next dc, 3 dc in next ch-1 sp, drop Color A, with second color, ch 1, 3 dc in same ch-1 sp, skip next 3 dc, 3 dc in sp **before** next dc, (3 dc, ch 1, 3 dc) in next ch-1 sp, skip next 3 dc, 3 dc in sp **before** next dc, 3 dc in same sp as first dc, ch 1; join with slip st to first dc, finish off leaving a long end for sewing.

ASSEMBLY

Using Chart as a guide, whipstitch Squares together to form strips *(Fig. 2, page 36)*. Join strips in same manner.

BORDER

With **right** side facing, join Color A with slip st in ch-1 sp at upper right corner; ch 3, 2 dc in same sp, ★ [skip next 3 dc, 3 dc in sp before next dc] twice, † 3 dc in each of next 2 ch-1 sps, [skip next 3 dc, 3 dc in sp **before** next dc] twice †, rep from † to † across to next corner ch-1 sp, (3 dc, ch 1, 3 dc) in next corner ch-1 sp; rep from ★ 2 times **more**; [skip next 3 dc, 3 dc in sp **before** next dc] twice; rep from † to † across to same sp as first dc, 3 dc in same sp as first dc, ch 1; join with slip st to first dc, finish off.

Love the colors of this afghan? Use them to make one of these variations.

Variations

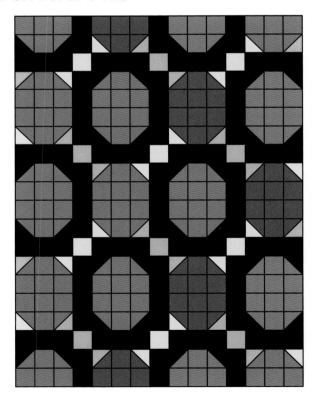

1

2

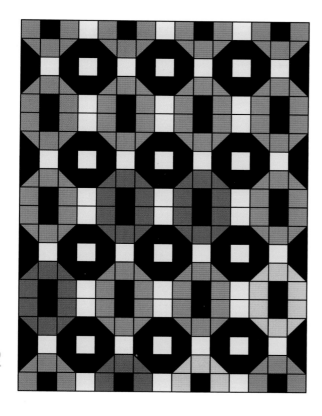

3

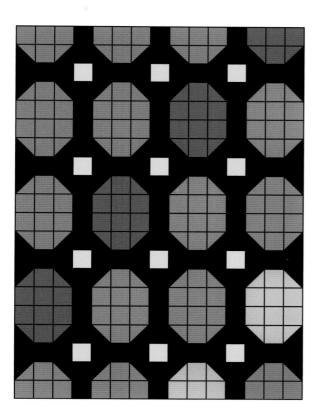

4

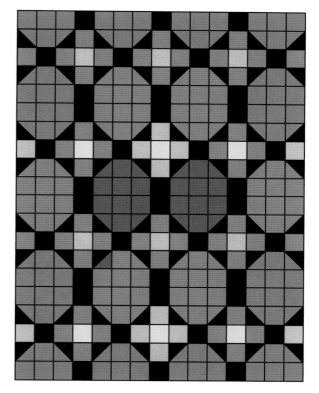

Puzzled

◖■▢▷ EASY

Finished Size: Approximately 49" x 61"
(124.5 cm x 155 cm)

MATERIALS
Medium Weight Yarn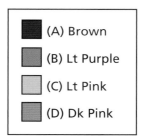
    [3.5 ounces, 210 yards
    (100 grams, 192 meters) per skein]:
        Brown (A) - 4 skeins
        Lt Purple (B) - 4 skeins
        Lt Pink (C) - 4 skeins
        Dk Pink (D) - 4 skeins
Crochet hook, size G (4 mm) **or** size needed
    for gauge
Yarn needle

GAUGE
One square = 3" (7.5 cm)

SQUARE
Make 76 with Color A, 87 with Color B, 91 with Color C and 66 with Color D.

Ch 4, join with a slip st to form a ring.

Rnd 1 (Right side): Ch 3 **(counts as first dc, now and throughout)**, 2 dc in ring; (ch 1, 3 dc in ring) 3 times; sc in first dc to form last ch-1 sp.

Rnd 2: Ch 3, 2 dc in last ch-1 sp made, ★ (3 dc, ch 1, 3 dc) in next ch-1 sp; rep from ★ 2 times **more**, 3 dc in same sp as first dc; sc in first dc to form last ch-1 sp.

Rnd 3: Ch 3, 2 dc in last ch-1 sp made, ★ skip next 3 dc, 3 dc in sp **before** next dc *(Fig. 1, page 36)*, (3 dc, ch 1, 3 dc) in next ch-1 sp; rep from ★ 2 times **more**, 3 dc in sp **before** next dc, 3 dc in same sp as first dc, ch 1; join with slip st to first dc, finish off leaving a long end for sewing.

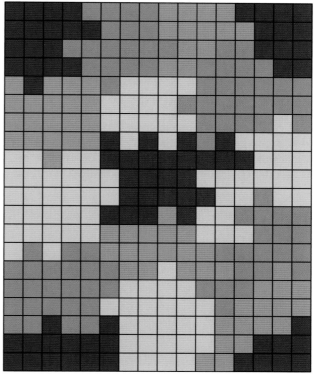

CHART   *16 x 20 squares*

COLOR KEY

■	(A) Brown
■	(B) Lt Purple
□	(C) Lt Pink
▣	(D) Dk Pink

ASSEMBLY

Using Chart as a guide, whipstitch Squares together to form strips *(Fig. 2, page 36)*. Join strips in same manner.

BORDER

With **right** side facing, join Color A with slip st in ch-1 sp at upper right corner; ch 3, 2 dc in same sp, ★ [skip next 3 dc, 3 dc in sp before next dc] twice, † 3 dc in each of next 2 ch-1 sps, [skip next 3 dc, 3dc in sp **before** next dc] twice †, rep from † to † across to next corner ch-1 sp, (3 dc, ch 1, 3 dc) in next corner ch-1 sp; rep from ★ 2 times **more**; [skip next 3 dc, 3 dc in sp **before** next dc] twice; rep from † to † across to same sp as first dc, 3 dc in same sp as first dc, ch 1; join with slip st to first dc, finish off.

Love the colors of this afghan? Use them to make one of these variations.

Variations

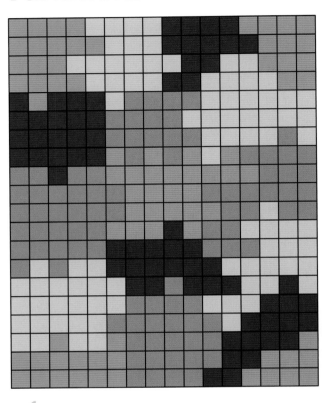

1

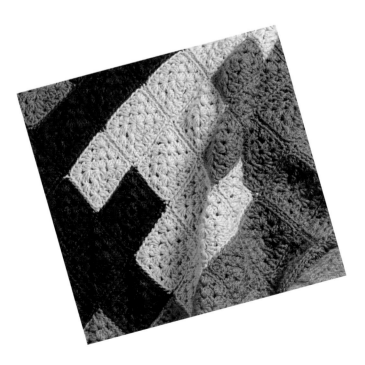

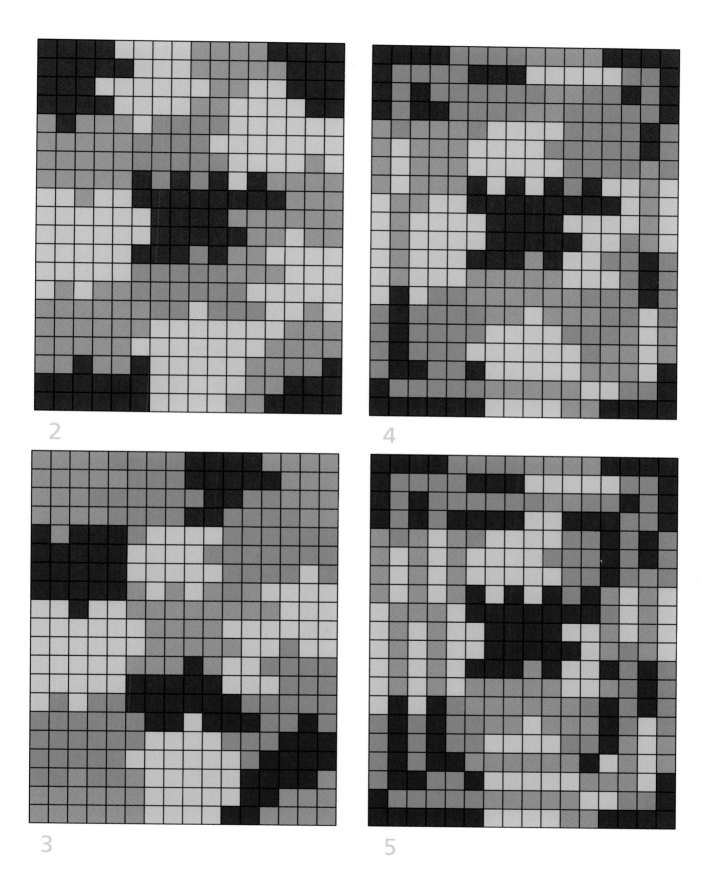

2

3

4

5

10

Belt Buckles

◖▮▢▷ **EASY**

Finished Size: Approximately 43" x 64"
(109 cm x 162.5 cm)

MATERIALS

Medium Weight Yarn ⑷
    [6 ounces, 278 yards
    (170 grams, 254 meters) per skein]:
        Black (A) - 3 skeins
        Yellow (B) - 3 skeins
        Brown (C) - 2 skeins
        Red (D) - 2 skeins
Crochet hook, size G (4 mm) **or** size needed
    for gauge
Yarn needle

GAUGE

One square = 3" (7.5 cm)

ONE-COLOR SQUARE

**Make 102 with Color A, 72 with Color B, 48 with
color C and 24 with Color D.**

Ch 4, join with a slip st to form a ring.

Rnd 1 (Right side): Ch 3 **(counts as first dc, now
and throughout)**, 2 dc in ring; (ch 1, 3 dc in ring)
3 times; sc in first dc to form last ch-1 sp.

Rnd 2: Ch 3, 2 dc in last ch-1 sp made, ★ (3 dc,
ch 1, 3 dc) in next ch-1 sp; rep from ★ 2 times
more, 3 dc in same sp as first dc; sc in first dc to
form last ch-1 sp.

Rnd 3: Ch 3, 2 dc in last ch-1 sp made, ★ skip next
3 dc, 3 dc in sp **before** next dc (*Fig. 1, page 36*),
(3 dc, ch 1, 3 dc) in next ch-1 sp; rep from ★
2 times **more**, 3 dc in sp **before** next dc, 3 dc in
same sp as first dc, ch 1; join with slip st to first dc,
finish off leaving a long end for sewing.

CHART   *14 x 21 squares*

COLOR KEY

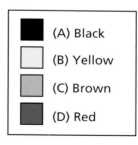

■ (A) Black
□ (B) Yellow
▨ (C) Brown
▩ (D) Red

TWO-COLOR SQUARE
Make 48 with Color B and Color D.

With Color D, ch 4, join with a slip st to form a ring.

Rnd 1 (Right side): Ch 3, 2 dc in ring, ch 1, 3 dc in ring; drop Color D, with Color B, ch 1, (3 dc, ch 1) twice in ring; join with slip st to first dc.

Rnd 2: With Color B, ch 3, turn; 2 dc in first ch-1 sp, (3 dc, ch 1, 3 dc) in next ch-1 sp, 3 dc in next ch-1 sp; drop Color B, with Color D, ch 1, 3 dc in same sp; (3 dc, ch 1, 3 dc) in next ch-1 sp, 3 dc in same sp as first dc, ch 1; join with slip st to first dc.

Rnd 3: With Color D, ch 3, turn; 2 dc in first ch-1 sp, skip next 3 dc, 3 dc in sp **before** next dc, (3 dc, ch 1, 3 dc) in next ch-1 sp, skip next 3 dc, 3 dc in sp **before** next dc, 3 dc in next ch-1 sp; drop Color D, with Color B, ch 1, 3 dc in same ch-1 sp, skip next 3 dc, 3 dc in sp **before** next dc, (3 dc, ch 1, 3 dc) in next ch-1 sp, skip next 3 dc, 3 dc in sp **before** next dc, 3 dc in same sp as first dc, ch 1; join with slip st to first dc, finish off leaving a long end for sewing.

ASSEMBLY
Using Chart as a guide, whipstitch Squares together to form strips (*Fig. 2, page 36*). Join strips in same manner.

BORDER
With **right** side facing, join Color D with slip st in ch-1 sp at upper right corner; ch 3, 2 dc in same sp, ★ [skip next 3 dc, 3 dc in sp before next dc] twice, † 3 dc in each of next 2 ch-1 sps, [skip next 3 dc, 3 dc in sp **before** next dc] twice †, rep from † to † across to next corner ch-1 sp, (3 dc, ch 1, 3 dc) in next corner ch-1 sp; rep from ★ 2 times **more**; [skip next 3 dc, 3 dc in sp **before** next dc] twice; rep from † to † across to same sp as first dc, 3 dc in same sp as first dc, ch 1; join with slip st to first dc, finish off.

Love the colors of this afghan? Use them to make one of these variations.

Variations

1

2

4

3

5

Greys on Pink

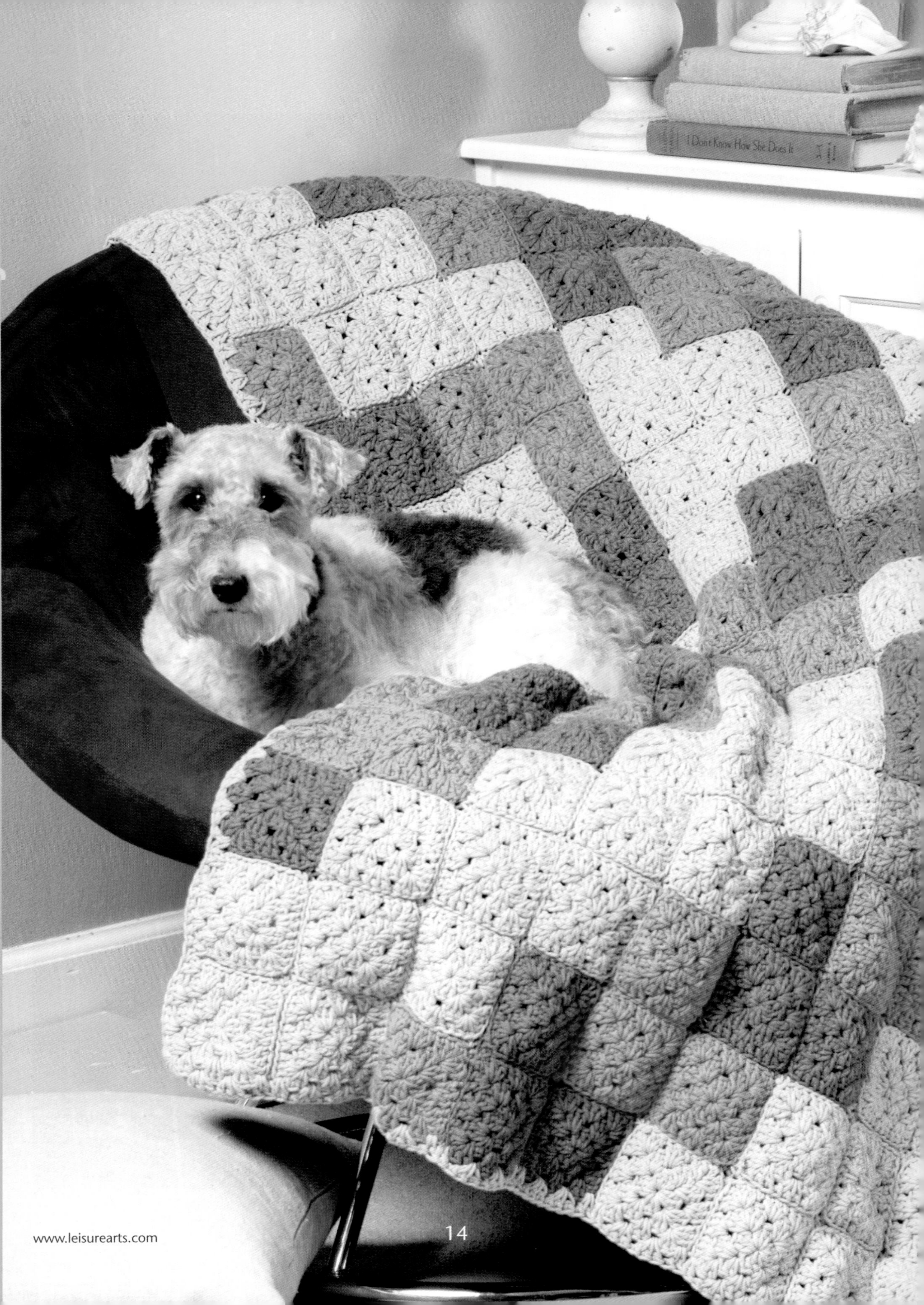

Greys on Pink

Finished Size: Approximately 49" x 67"
(124.5 cm x 170 cm)

MATERIALS
Medium Weight Yarn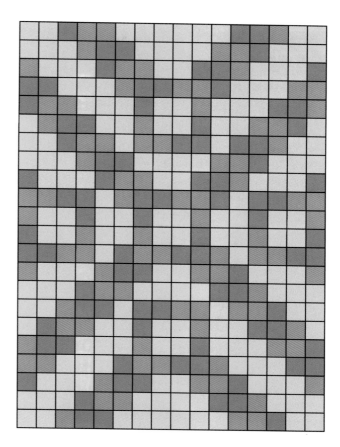
    [3.5 ounces, 207 yards
    (100 grams, 188 meters) per ball]:
        Lt Grey (A) - 10 balls
        Dk Grey (B) - 6 balls
        Pink (C) - 6 balls
Crochet hook, size G (4 mm) **or** size needed
    for gauge
Yarn needle

GAUGE
One Square = 3" (7.5 cm)

SQUARE
**Make 172 with Color A, 90 with Color B and
90 with Color C.**

Ch 4, join with a slip st to form a ring.

Rnd 1 (Right side): Ch 3 (**counts as first dc, now
and throughout**), 2 dc in ring; (ch 1, 3 dc in ring) 3
times; sc in first dc to form last ch-1 sp.

Rnd 2: Ch 3, 2 dc in last ch-1 sp made, ★ (3 dc,
ch 1, 3 dc) in next ch-1 sp; rep from ★ 2 times
more, 3 dc in same sp as first dc; sc in first dc to
form last ch-1 sp.

Rnd 3: Ch 3, 2 dc in last ch-1 sp made, ★ skip next
3 dc, 3 dc in sp **before** next dc (*Fig. 1, page 36*),
(3 dc, ch 1, 3 dc) in next ch-1 sp; rep from ★
2 times **more**, 3 dc in sp **before** next dc, 3 dc in
same sp as first dc, ch 1; join with slip st to first dc,
finish off leaving a long end for sewing.

CHART   *16 x 22 squares*

COLOR KEY

⬜	(A) Lt Grey
⬛	(B) Dk Grey
⬛	(C) Pink

ASSEMBLY

Using Chart as a guide, whipstitch Squares together to form strips *(Fig. 2, page 36)*. Join strips in same manner.

BORDER

With **right** side facing, join Color A with slip st in ch-1 sp at upper right corner; ch 3, 2 dc in same sp, ★ [skip next 3 dc, 3 dc in sp before next dc] twice, † 3 dc in each of next 2 ch-1 sps, [skip next 3 dc, 3 dc in sp **before** next dc] twice †, rep from † to † across to next corner ch-1 sp, (3 dc, ch 1, 3 dc) in next corner ch-1 sp; rep from ★ 2 times **more**; [skip next 3 dc, 3 dc in sp **before** next dc] twice; rep from † to † across to same sp as first dc, 3 dc in same sp as first dc, ch 1; join with slip st to first dc, finish off.

Love the colors of this afghan? Use them to make one of these variations.

Variations

1

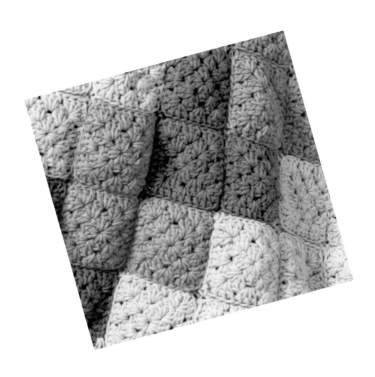

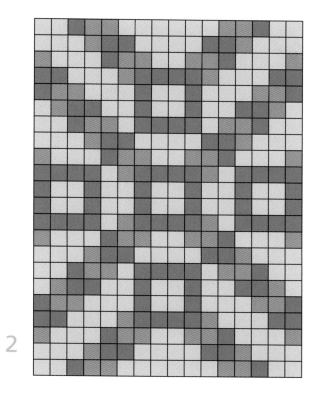

2

4

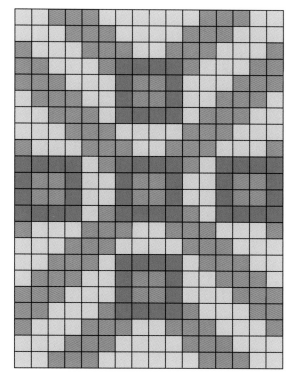

3

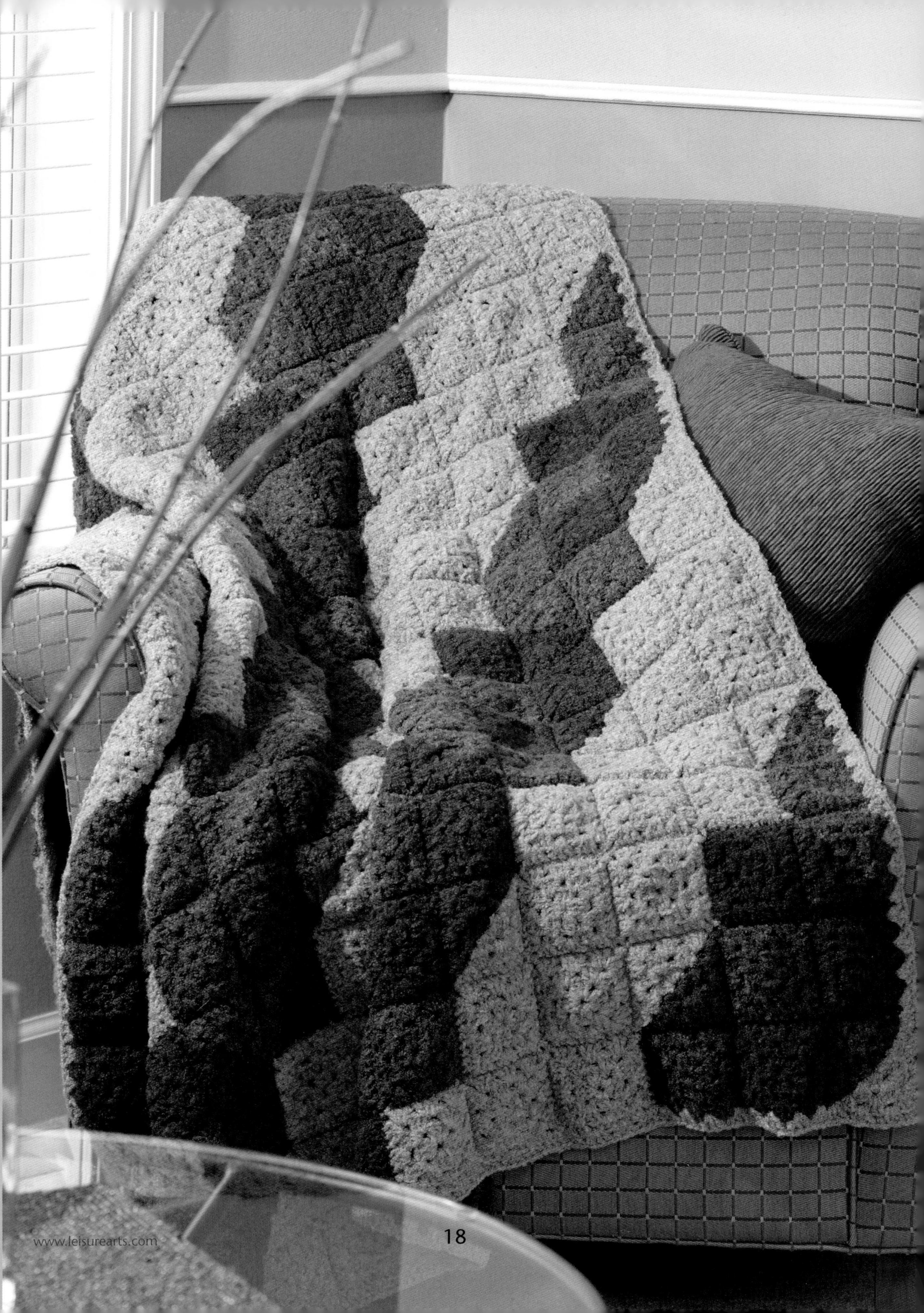

Five C's

EASY

Finished Size: Approximately 46" x 61"
(117 cm x 155 cm)

MATERIALS
Medium Weight Yarn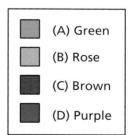
    [6 ounces, 278 yards
    (170 grams, 254 meters) per skein]:
        Green (A) - 3 skeins
        Rose (B) - 3 skeins
        Brown (C) - 3 skeins
        Purple (D) - 3 skeins
Crochet hook, size G (4 mm) **or** size needed
    for gauge
Yarn needle

GAUGE
One Square = 3" (7.5 cm)

ONE-COLOR SQUARE
Make 55 each with Colors A, B, C, and D.

Ch 4, join with a slip st to form a ring.

Rnd 1 (Right side): Ch 3 **(counts as first dc, now and throughout)**, 2 dc in ring; (ch 1, 3 dc in ring) 3 times; sc in first dc to form last ch-1 sp.

Rnd 2: Ch 3, 2 dc in last ch-1 sp made, ★ (3 dc, ch 1, 3 dc) in next ch-1 sp; rep from ★ 2 times more, 3 dc in same sp as first dc; sc in first dc to form last ch-1 sp.

Rnd 3: Ch 3, 2 dc in last ch-1 sp made, ★ skip next 3 dc, 3 dc in sp **before** next dc (*Fig. 1, page 36*), (3 dc, ch 1, 3 dc) in next ch-1 sp; rep from ★ 2 times **more**, 3 dc in sp **before** next dc, 3 dc in same sp as first dc, ch 1; join with slip st to first dc, finish off leaving a long end for sewing.

CHART   *15 x 20 squares*

COLOR KEY

▦	(A) Green
▦	(B) Rose
▦	(C) Brown
▦	(D) Purple

TWO-COLOR SQUARE

Make 20 with Colors D and C, 20 with Colors D and B, 20 with Colors A and B, and 20 with Colors A and C.

With first color, ch 4, join with a slip st to form a ring.

Rnd 1 (Right side): Ch 3, 2 dc in ring, ch 1, 3 dc in ring; drop first color, with second color, ch 1, (3 dc, ch 1) twice in ring; join with slip st to first dc.

Rnd 2: With second color, ch 3, turn; 2 dc in first ch-1 sp, (3 dc, ch 1, 3 dc) in next ch-1 sp, 3 dc in next ch-1 sp; drop second color, with first color, ch 1, 3 dc in same sp, (3 dc, ch 1, 3 dc) in next ch-1 sp, 3 dc in same sp as first dc, ch 1; join with slip st to first dc.

Rnd 3: With first color, ch 3, turn; 2 dc in first ch-1 sp, skip next 3 dc, 3 dc in sp **before** next dc, (3 dc, ch 1, 3 dc) in next ch-1 sp, skip next 3 dc, 3 dc in sp **before** next dc, 3 dc in next ch-1 sp; drop first color, with second color, ch 1, 3 dc in same ch-1 sp, skip next 3 dc, 3 dc in sp **before** next dc, (3 dc, ch 1, 3 dc) in next ch-1 sp, skip next 3 dc, 3 dc in sp **before** next dc, 3 dc in same sp as first dc, ch 1; join with slip st to first dc, finish off leaving a long end for sewing.

ASSEMBLY

Using Chart as a guide, whipstitch Squares together to form strips *(Fig. 2, page 36)*. Join strips in same manner.

BORDER

With **right** side facing, join Color B with slip st in ch-1 sp at upper right corner; ch 3, 2 dc in same sp, ★ [skip next 3 dc, 3 dc in sp before next dc] twice, † 3 dc in each of next 2 ch-1 sps, [skip next 3 dc, 3 dc in sp **before** next dc] twice †, rep from † to † across to next corner ch-1 sp, (3 dc, ch 1, 3 dc) in next corner ch-1 sp; rep from ★ 2 times **more**; [skip next 3 dc, 3 dc in sp **before** next dc] twice; rep from † to † across to same sp as first dc, 3 dc in same sp as first dc, ch 1; join with slip st to first dc, finish off.

Love the colors of this afghan? Use them to make one of these variations.

Variations

1

2

3

4

Echoes

14 x 20 squares

COLOR KEY

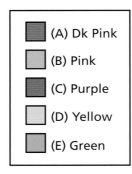

(A) Dk Pink

(B) Pink

(C) Purple

(D) Yellow

(E) Green

Variations

1

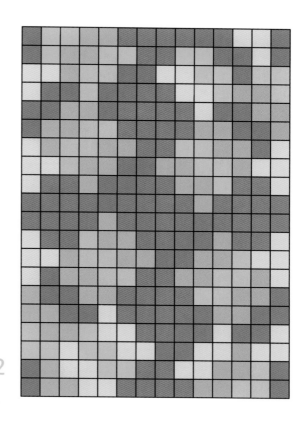

2

3

23

English Garden

16 x 20 squares

COLOR KEY

- (A) Olive Green
- (B) Cream
- (C) Lt Rose
- (C) Violet

Variations

1

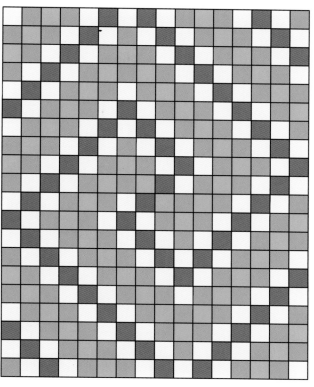

2

3

25

Barrel of Monkeys

16 x 20 squares

COLOR KEY

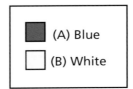

(A) Blue

(B) White

Variations

1

2

3

27

Flower Power

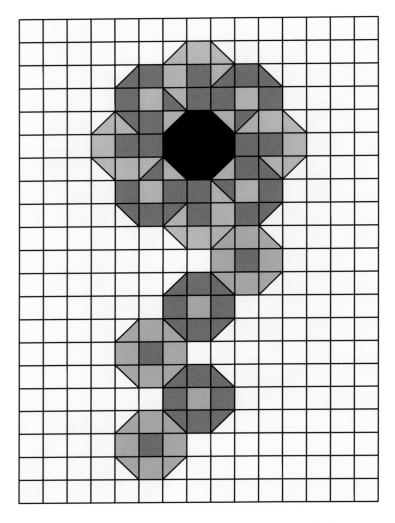

15 x 21 squares

COLOR KEY

- ☐ (A) White
- ▨ (B) Green
- ▨ (C) Dk Green
- ▨ (D) Pink
- ▨ (E) Purple
- ■ (F) Black

Variations

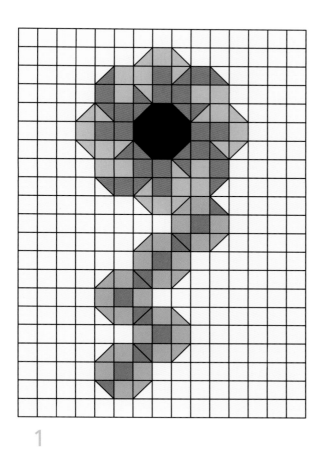

1

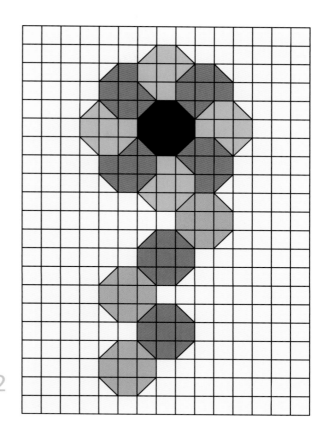

2

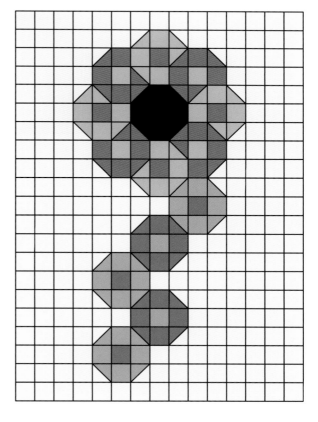

3

29

Southwest

16 x 20 squares

COLOR KEY

■	(A) Green
■	(B) Red
■	(C) Purple
□	(D) Yellow

Variations

1

2

3

31

Zigzag

15 x 21 squares

COLOR KEY

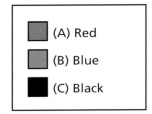

(A) Red

(B) Blue

(C) Black

Variations

1

2

3

General Instructions

ABBREVIATIONS

ch(s)	chain(s)
cm	centimeter
dc	double crochet
mm	millimeter
Rnd(s)	round(s)
sc	single crochet
sp(s)	space(s)
st(s)	stitch(es)

★ — work instructions following ★ as many **more** times as indicated in addition to the first time.

( ) or [ ] — work enclosed instructions **as many** times as specified by the number immediately following **or** work all enclosed instructions in the stitch or space indicated **or** contains explanatory remarks.

† to † — work all instructions from first † to second † **as many** times as specified.

GAUGE

Exact gauge is **essential** for proper size. Before beginning your project, make a sample swatch in the yarn and hook specified. After completing the swatch, measure it, counting your rounds carefully. If your swatch is larger or smaller than specified, **make another, changing hook size to get the correct gauge.** Keep trying until you find the size hook that will give you the specified gauge.

WORKING IN A SPACE BEFORE A STITCH

When instructed to work in a space **before** a stitch or in spaces **between** stitches, insert hook in space indicated by arrow *(Fig. 1)*.

WHIPSTITCH

Place two Squares with **wrong** sides together. Beginning in ch-1 sp, sew through both pieces once to secure the beginning of the seam, leaving an ample yarn end to weave in later. Working through **inside** loops of each stitch on **both** pieces, insert the needle from **front** to **back** through first stitch and pull yarn through *(Fig. 2)*, ★ insert the needle from **front** to **back** through next stitch and pull yarn through; repeat from ★ across.

Fig. 1

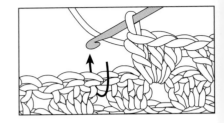

Fig. 2

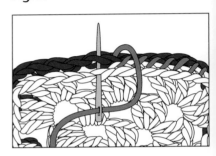

CROCHET TERMINOLOGY

UNITED STATES		INTERNATIONAL
slip stitch (slip st)	=	single crochet (sc)
single crochet (sc)	=	double crochet (dc)
half double crochet (hdc)	=	half treble crochet (htr)
double crochet (dc)	=	treble crochet(tr)
treble crochet (tr)	=	double treble crochet (dtr)
double treble crochet (dtr)	=	triple treble crochet (ttr)
triple treble crochet (tr tr)	=	quadruple treble crochet (qtr)
skip	=	miss

CROCHET HOOKS

U.S.	B-1	C-2	D-3	E-4	F-5	G-6	H-8	I-9	J-10	K-10½	N	P	Q
Metric - mm	2.25	2.75	3.25	3.5	3.75	4	5	5.5	6	6.5	9	10	15

Yarn Weight Symbol & Names	LACE 0	SUPER FINE 1	FINE 2	LIGHT 3	MEDIUM 4	BULKY 5	SUPER BULKY 6
Type of Yarns in Category	Fingering, 10-count crochet thread	Sock, Fingering Baby	Sport, Baby	DK, Light Worsted	Worsted, Afghan, Aran	Chunky, Craft, Rug	Bulky, Roving
Crochet Gauge* Ranges in Single Crochet to 4" (10 cm)	32-42 double crochets**	21-32 sts	16-20 sts	12-17 sts	11-14 sts	8-11 sts	5-9 sts
Advised Hook Size Range	Steel*** 6,7,8 Regular hook B-1	B-1 to E-4	E-4 to 7	7 to I-9	I-9 to K-10.5	K-10.5 to M-13	M-13 and larger

*GUIDELINES ONLY: The chart above reflects the most commonly used gauges and hook sizes for specific yarn categories.

** Lace weight yarns are usually crocheted on larger-size hooks to create lacy openwork patterns. Accordingly, a gauge range is difficult to determine. Always follow the gauge stated in your pattern.

*** Steel crochet hooks are sized differently from regular hooks–the higher the number the smaller the hook, which is the reverse of regular hook sizing.

◼◻◻◻ BEGINNER	Projects for first-time crocheters using basic stitches. Minimal shaping.
◼◼◻◻ EASY	Projects using yarn with basic stitches, repetitive stitch patterns, simple color changes, and simple shaping and finishing.
◼◼◼◻ INTERMEDIATE	Projects using a variety of techniques, such as basic lace patterns or color patterns, mid-level shaping and finishing.
◼◼◼◼ EXPERIENCED	Projects with intricate stitch patterns, techniques and dimension, such as non-repeating patterns, multi-color techniques, fine threads, small hooks, detailed shaping and refined finishing.

Yarn Information

The afghans in this leaflet were made using medium weight yarn. Any brand of medium weight yarn may be used. It is best to refer to the yardage/meters when determining how many balls or skeins to purchase. Remember, to arrive at the finished size, it is the GAUGE/TENSION that is most important, not the brand of yarn. For your convenience, listed below are the specific yarns used to create our photography models.

PAINTED EGGS
Lion Brand® Wool-Ease®
Color A - #153 Black
Color B - #191 Violet
Color C - #139 Dk Rose Heather
Color D - #195 Azalea Pink
Color E - #138 Cranberry
Color F - #102 Ranch Red
Color G - #188 Paprika
Color H - #171 Gold
Color I - #157 Pastel Yellow

PUZZLED
Patons® Décor
Color A - #87633 Chocolate Taupe
Color B - #87309 New Lilac
Color C - #87433 New Rose
Color D - #87436 Rose Temptation

BELT BUCKLES
TLC® Amore™
Color A - #3002 Black
Color B - #3005 Sand
Color D - #3907 Red Velvet
Red Heart® Plush™
*Color C - #9104 Taupe

GREYS ON PINK
Lion Brand® Cotton-Ease®
Color A - #149 Stone
Color B - #122 Taupe
Color C - #112 Berry

FIVE C'S
TLC®Amore™
Color A - #3627 Lt Thyme
*Color B - #3710 Rose
*Color C - #3324 Chocolate
*Color D - #3534 Plum

*Yarn color/brand may no longer be available. We are sorry for any inconvenience.

Produced by Creative Partners™, LLC

Production Team
Creative Directors: Jean Leinhauser and Rita Weiss
Charts: Linda Causee
Book Design: Joyce Lerner
Pattern Testers:
  Tracy Pokrzywa, Saint Charles, Missouri
  Marsha Sieber, Sweet Home, Oregon
  Carrie Cristiano, Escondido, California
  Jennifer Marr, Edmond, Oklahoma

LEISURE ARTS®
the art of everyday living
www.leisurearts.com

Production Team
Technical Writer/Editor: Joan Beebe, Jean Guirguis and Peggy Greig
Editorial Writer: Susan McManus Johnson
Senior Graphic Artist: Lora Puls
Graphic Artist: Jane Fay
Photography Manager: Katherine Laughlin
Photo Stylist: Sondra Daniel
Photographer: Ken West

We have made every effort to ensure that these instructions are accurate and complete. We cannot, however, be responsible for human error, typographical mistakes, or variations in individual work.